Free Verse Editions

Edited by Jon Thompson

Praise for *At The Edge Of Forever* by Angel Elisa Collier

"*At The Edge Of Forever* inhabits a landscape where humans hum with each color and hymn of the natural world. Each bird, dream and cloud quilt will hold your breath in beauty. Angel Elisa Collier writes from a big sky. Paws trespass your arm, the trees and breathe out of the forest. This is the perfect book to read after a hectic day and your entire being craves beauty."

— Lisha Adela García, Author of *A Rope of Luna*

"Heaven opens its blue book of psalms and the reader opens a bit of heaven in this new collection by Angel Elisa Collier. With images that burrow into the reader's mind, her words continue to pulse long after the reader puts down the book. Her work is brilliant; I loved immersing myself in it."

— KB Ballentine, Author of *The Light Tears Loose*

"Angel Elisa Collier's *At The Edge Of Forever* finds entrances in Nature for our human spirit. Translucence and transcendence, the search for a sanctuary. Even a falling leaf is a sanctuary, one that endures."

— Ken Pobo, Author of *Bend of Quiet*

"Angel Elisa Collier's poems are exotic butterflies. Lovely language, vision, beauty, a spiritual connection with the land, the birds, and the trees. Her poems reveal a divine tenderness, an honest telling, an open diary of her life and soul. Her language sings and shines."

— Diane Frank, Author of *Canon for Bears and Ponderosa Pines*

"Filled with visions and landscapes, Angel Elisa Collier's second book is a testament to her family, the places of her home, her strong connection to the ineffable. Her poems bring me to the edge of forever, and I find myself wrapped in the feathers of her hope. What an amazing voice she offers this world."

— Betsy Snider, Author of *Hope is a Muscle*

THE BOOK OF ISAAC

Aidan Semmens

Parlor Press
Anderson, South Carolina
www.parlorpress.com

Parlor Press LLC, Anderson, South Carolina, 29621

Library of Congress Cataloging-in-Publication Data

Semmens, Aidan.
  The book of Isaac / Aidan Semmens.
      pages. cm. -- (Free verse editions)
  Includes bibliographical references.
  ISBN 978-1-60235-373-2 (pbk. : alk. paper) -- ISBN 978-1-
60235-374-9 (Adobe ebook) -- ISBN 978-1-60235-375-6 (epub)
  I. Title. II. Series: Free verse editions.
  PR6069.E395B66 2013
  821'.914--dc23
                                                2012044928

Cover design by David Blakesley.
Cover photograph provided by the author.

Printed on acid-free paper.

Parlor Press, LLC is an independent publisher of scholarly and
trade titles in print and multimedia formats. This book is available
in paperback and ebook formats from Parlor Press on the World
Wide Web at http://www.parlorpress.com or through online and
brick-and-mortar bookstores. For submission information or to
find out about Parlor Press publications, write to Parlor Press,
3015 Brackenberry Drive, Anderson, South Carolina, 29621, or
email editor@parlorpress.com.

For IAH & all the subsequent Hourwiches

Contents

Contents

THE BOOK OF ISAAC

this Esdras went up from Babylon as a scribe
& they feasted with instruments of music & of gladness
& roasted the Passover with fire as appertaineth
& such a Passover was not kept in Israel since
the time of the prophet Samuel; as for the house
of the Lord they burnt it, & brake down the walls of Jerusalem
& set fire upon her towers, now if this city
& the walls thereof be re-made they will also rebel
against kings for ye have defiled your hands with blood
the evil is sown but the destruction is not yet come
& we are not better than they that there did die
they that dwell upon the earth may understand nothing
& as for the truth it endureth as is always strong
for the world has lost his youth & the times wax old

bent writing, assiduous pen in hand,
beard unknowing as mine, a man
dead decades before underlies
by one eighth my genesis
in a twilight era from rabbinical composition
under secular thought logic
to weigh the weight of fire
pioneer of mill-ground clothworkers
farmers in a barrier of road escape
from hard land sweaty life, heretic
suffers no holy writ gladly
in vernacular of old places, the family left
to control of the secret police & he returns
pose, the unknowable, Minsk 1907

radicalism is not your mistake
your tub is a poison & the stink of later
is very deep dark & all unseen
the name of a flower is the name
of something else, respected citizens
First Guild merchant of hereditary noble
it is difficult to dismiss corrupt ideas
Thermidor & the rotten smell exuded
a moral concern for the betterment of all
when conflict between leaders & location
each side accusing the other of conspiracy
of the revolution's betrayal
the privileges are granted bourgeois experts
& tillers per plant from the soil & stood as one

for them many living on the earth
the sway of famine & those that flee
destroy the sword; the dead will be deported
as dung, unmourned, for the earth be desolate sorrow,
threw down the cities, would no one be left
even to the laying of the ground, will give fruit trees
& who will pick? grapes will ripen
& who walk on them? Adam we will see
as another to hear his voice, is the city
will be televised on ten & two in the field, hidden
in the thick woods & in crevices of stone;
as olives cling to a tree through winter,
a few shall remain living witness to the sword search
& machineguns distort the house of prayer

our psaltery is laid down on the land,
our song for silencing, joy in an extremity,
our light of candle out, the coffer of our ruined obligation
depending on the refuge of our contracts
become useless holy things & the column you marched;
the name we tell are rottenly used, the children
placed with us in shame; our priest is burnt,
our Levites in captivity virgins are,
do our spouses charm, befouled, she religiously observed,
chose to cover her hair, brought new men in subjection
strong made weak & our great seal of Sion
set in the hands of those which hate;
honoured house when Gaon conducted prayer
is demolished, relieved to the level with our despair

expound, expound, the vinestocks lie untended
our scarlet flower is cast on the stone-white stone
in the mirror of memory have been said that I radically
rendered bone of our bone, instructed between we then
prayed a sickly prayer to the violent dead woman
witness the courageous slashing themselves with blades
time is the evil, evil, a day & a day
that after famine called back all the people
to evil & further evil, a curse cursed on our children
the huntress in broken plaster keeps vigil no longer
on the haze-misted breasts of Helen in the ghetto
descending of Aaron in which the other war
a man is dead, another one decomposed, a dull end
& the life ignites, moon shining on naked hills

as for us & of art & art, you have expressed, beauty
to arouse under which the least suspicions will expect
of a darkened sun, an illustration of the bright jets
was covered, bent, up to now far away from the dark
that does commit to us, complete, in our fathers;
as for mathematics, on the other hand & of the eye
grave of the human seen from the earth – the wall
& which the tree becomes, the stove & where the paint tree
the punishment thing takes off & ecstatic falls,
inoperative child & torn, rejected, all its unwept
& rips in the ritual conjunct where carries all sins
which the pillar of Abraham reaches great climax
was calculated installation installed
authentic opinion is impossible to restore

I conducted you through & sea, at the beginning
gave to you soft passage, Moshe for the leader of
& Aaron for the priest; I gave to you light
in the fire, great interests they have made I among you,
but for forgot me & is triumphed not in my name
for destroying your enemies; I had a pity on your mournings,
gave to you a bread of angels, cleft the rock for your water,
covered you with leaves; I shared among you the fruitful earth,
he threw outside those that squandered there,
evicted from their homes & families
legal conflict for property rights debating
but you blaspheme my name, would not obey
the poet who composed the Torah as a soldier might,
believing in concrete truths, absolute & absolve

as if by you requested I shall not hear
at any time your hand which has the blood to commit
your foot slaughter was quick & made unclean, you are not,
were it like, the writing as each one your oneself go back on;
now when you provide I will rotate my face to go
your solemn feast meal crescent moon, your circumcisions
I revoke; I dispatched to your mine prophet, you kill, bodily
their organism tears from your hand which demands their blood;
your house is desolate, chilly wind the stump will expel
one as you, your children the fruit is not opened
was the thing plentifully, badly despised the commanded work;
your houses are communicated to a people yet to come
in order to witness will decrease believing
certified who small they with faith are glad for gladness

intention of the blower is critical to hearer
if mitzvah is legitimate, if perhaps he stands still
& the intentionally burned through horn hears for the command
held, to be fulfilled the person, who should the shofar
on Rosh Hashanah in Torah is likewise learned
fear of the God of the ram of a cloud leaks out
to the ancient, those on the verge, too smitten
with reverence in order perhaps it is thought to tremble
the horn announces the seventh month, Tishri the first day
you will oversleep from your moral sleep
it finished there to be Sanhedrin
& your conduct searches which become best
you can, shall investigate fearfully,
shofar should not sound in Shabbat

in shul & bes-medresh we occupy these text
this connection we, fully on the longing,
to our fathers (yea, & ye mothers also),
the cross-over canyon from the dream, cannot rise
in the bilateral frightened dreamer's life
to our fathers' fathers' desire: it is not we so are interested
in physics & mathematics, rather this Einstein
is the sign we crave of present life to look
that uses grave & upwardly from earth's naked eye
to use the star report the heaven blood so far,
a sun's strange glimpsing which eclipses,
a strange flash of shaded helium, picture of bent light beams,
removed up to now from the dreary oppressive
of life, dreams float in air, shtetl visions of Chagall

the woodcarving tradition which delivers
at the duration of centuries reached
at a formidable climax in the throne of Solomon
carved in many components by Aaron Chait from Kelmé,
that life, which is transferred in regard to love,
a very sculptural incorporation of architectural elements,
animals & representation in more than 200 dolls
had mounted in the one cut & scholar, to gather on behalf
of the character at court unwise by wise & formidable kings
extended via biblical histories & popular fable;
as for that kind of constitution, the secure view
which the enormous frequency of current scarcity
is not known with history of art divides
with cause becoming as before, impossible

in order not to break the second command
threatening representation of human form
that reputation is given to the god which is limited
to the former form of art; synagogue & which comprehends;
ritual object; respects a family holiday in ceremony,
which have the mosaic tablet of the circular law
arched double doors of the ark in a house of refuge
ahead the cartouche of prayer, the ritual candlestick
from before the cantor's desk, these objects all is left;
the large house where cultural hegemony,
community above was grasped, the expression
which is artistic specifies – is complicated, precisely,
this aron kodesh, finely contrived & perished exquisitely
with & of the synagogues; its peoples

the input viewpoint takes truth ignorant & in disguise;
savage, the deceit is the revenge
the redness of the finger plunged in wine
under cannibal ritual of the masticated body
assumed son of the author served as bread
is transposed on the blameless in their midst
which is pricked out for humiliation,
malicious fiction of good poisoned innocently
appointed to the role of suffering in reprisal
punctured for degradation, the evil surrogate
here the unreliable narrator conjures Cyrus
tolerant prophet, doyen of the virtuous
elder of fair founder of return, the temple's sponsor
in Damascus that the Christian should wear yellow

fair reader's desire of the girl's capital
occupants captivating sky-blue eyes
lured back to Petersburg's fatal
never led to know my quarrel with the Romanov house
while I am prisoned she sent word
I needed her to call me in my breeding
comply with political rule of visiting
she pretext I & were
& indicated to pretend sympathy's excitement
the word love never was between us
the man certainly not as much fate I think myself
to reject her extraordinary kindness thanking her
for fear engagement with police
never again seen once we crossed the road & broke

Kropotkin settled with a sense of ease in silence
afforded scientific books & journals that he wrote every day
until sunset the structure of his time fortified by the bell
for worsening conditions like Isaac
a minute or two you did not see darkness so deep
Sergei Kravchinski reports cold chilling to the bone
damp mildew smell in one corner charnelhouse as a
straw bed with paperthin cover in another high
wooden pail that will poison your own stench
no books paper or soap but parasites
for eight & a half months our 19-year-old hero
imminent execution interred in his fear or exile
smuggling in the journal to read the death of Rozovsky
& believe that a writer his the more serious crime

an imperial world's population change
by law to negotiate the maze of unfair path
is impossible accurately to determine time
orthodox conspiracy against Holy Russian myth
becomes available in a hostile crowd
our Isaac jailed in Piter
said from a superior employee expects no release
because Jewish is considered for disruption especially
Josef Rozovsky is difficult to evade impression
in Kiev who knew the students of the school
hanged in dissemination of the People's Will
while proposal of his comrade sentence in the work of six years
were first victim of bigoted bureaucracy
intruders in the criminal justice polity

the schizoid character of Russian society
presented by a variety of self-
ranking by social estate &: honorary citizen,
Heritage Guild & the first base, trade,
state adviser, stockbroker, mechanical engineer,
woman doctor, director of the company, noble dentist
intelligence does not see herself
an elite a united group as classless
better for all concerned by moral dilemma
capacity to engage in critical thought
are often underutilised under education
ethos of commitment to serve the people
it is a very natural revolution
& end in disappointment disillusion

& masquerade of revellers; you will carry out to Purim
in proportion to death as a man who brandishes his sickle
beyond the head of a boy, which with hood & bearded
does represent perhaps a rabbi or unwise elder,
eliminates the procession, do not tear
your eye from the body which is severed,
dismembered hatred in Kishinev –
wooden walls & peeling colour of room,
wood combustion smoky stove & the bare floor
robbed, devastated mother & ravaged,
dead child torn; gives up, possessing their tear unwept –
nearby the bridge, in the road, in the crossing,
in the mud by the river ritual prayer of Rosh Hashanah
is observed: the water takes all, even so the sins

sound of blows began the dream of Vera
threatening fancy violent unknown threats
thrown around things, buildings cancelled
invisible hand, for unknown reasons & voice
loud, uncivil, savage voices, & worse
calm authority & submission tone
awake, under ceiling of the familiar, she hears
sounds & more terrible than before
that the voice between management & screaming, of course
she's the mother? & other more unfamiliar yet
it is the man, those men, depression next to it
still warm marked lack of Manya from the bed
the first clear words she hears – her own or Manya's?
the police came & mother left

Białystok from London on the reading & critique of Talmud
one workshop dealt with mass production of intellectuals
the Lower East Side brims over new people dynamically
no beer, but lectures, the venue does not provide free
public places, clubs & cafés full of the liveliest argument
in the social sphere, which is something like a public opinion formed
these young people, mostly immigrants, the Yiddish language was still
in dark nasty sweatshop, the cellars & attics in damp airless
ideology at odds with the old traditions imported
of paternalism and religion – in America the child rears the parent
guilty of intellectual property discourse, the language is Russian
must engage with the people & to do must master their tongue
maskilim & socialists as pin their faith education
redemption is found purely in secular knowledge

the café is the universities from the ghetto
on the Monopole on Second Avenue
& Ninth Street the issue once & Leon Trotsky
in the flesh, the meat, in a café Royale on Second & 12th
for a penny (& nickel tip) can be glass
tea & coffee pie while screening
the celebrity culture of Yiddish
fiddler Ferenc Miklós move gypsy & play
creator of dictionaries Alex Harkavy
Abraham Liessen, *Di Tsukunft* editor
Jacob Gordin, playwrights, all in heavy dark
Paley editor, economist Gurvich –
everywhere I meet people ready to fight
for what they believe & not believe in fighting

bay mir bistu sheyn, to me are you
so beautiful; on Second Avenue
the curtain rises, enter the greenhorn
yidishe meydel, object of our scorn
& mirth, our lust for the shtetl-born,
she brings fresh air in songs
love inconstancy & wrongs
that struck her cynical swain
father or severe again
we participate in laughter, happy tears
peel off to leave behind our plight & fear
haunts our night & day since we were here
teeters boundaries between chutzpah & pity
this fear of drowning in a foreign city

my dear Vladimir Ilyich, forgive that I do not address you as comrade,
I am pleased to send you this copy of my book a little
I hope that in your deliberations
the case of peasants fitness & do not forget
is in a village far from civilization
urbanization & your proletariat
nor in the smoky attic of intellectuals
beat dirty mind oppressed Russian
you & I want to girl pretending to earth bearing roses
& sustaining a position on Hegel's dialectic
but sleeping in the house where the stove babushka
& the icon of St Basil grimaces behind the door
hope all is good stout boots & coat
& a promise to maintain the crop year

the Russian peasant family alone
is a communistic commonwealth, where
population thin & undeveloped land
free, does not make sense to occupy large estates
not as impressive a peasant labour
increased private ownership of land
limits of the village community of domain
thus, land in the community without
communism & perfect domestic
Russia at the dawn of the fundamental period
the early history of land protection
hand in hand with personal dependence
wheel of landless earth unfed
the employer implies the employee

Gleb Oospensky in his suspicion stood alone
opposed his ironic smile to the illusion
the statistical inspector built farm diagrams
numbers in the report having no real value
the peasantist of the 70s whose opinions
were under influence by European thought
not to know that a kind of antagonism
is limited in the orders of peasantry
consider it a completely closed
the exploiter – *kulak* or *miroyed* –
& his victim a communistic peasant:
kulak means 'fist', miroyed 'peace fretter'
soubriquets of the usurer & landlord
the reality is the opposite case

no wise ruler the shepherd of his flock?
the farmer of stock placing his animals to mate
after the individual tendency release
which does not consider their mutual love considers decrease
of development after emancipation
in liberation will not later have defeat
who did not know how to influence
the archaic dissolution of the cell
of the commune of composite family became the evil of day
in the peasantist regarding will decline in the vill
of these archaic pillars with the deep regret of age-long
despotism of the elders began unendurable
woman of championed fight for individualism
to so use the term Michailovsky adopted

for me & not only for me in those days
that summons disbelief & animosity
for any faith in the higher degree of fanaticism
it become hard for with did I pass any bes medresh
without gnashing teeth & I could hardly be myself
to hear the voices of persons in prayer
or the study a page of Talmud, my largest delight
stood in demonstration that Moses did not write Torah
that Joshua did not make sun & the attitude of moons still
in tribute at the station to David no fine person
& Solomon his son no wise –
I make pause to illuminate heretical cigarettes
in the light of a candle to write on the Sabbath
in the sky of the earth, this realm is as accurate

to suffer silence is to suffer as a fool
massacre & poor impossible will
be God's will, tsar's deconstruction
is clearly the goal submergence
the turn of fully passionate desire
the young poet utopia earnestly
in the revolutionary's blood from the future
farmer & worker, soil & intelligence tiller supports
& mutually, equally basic as Turgenev is counter still
their radical false, the individual contribution
a leading role in radicalism
or remain aliens even when stuffed
with education as a pomegranate with seeds:
if this is thus, what point of God?

the first edition of Leviathan
is an image of a giant with a sword
& stick bishop towering above the ground
towns & villages, castles & churches
all visible body contains
myriad minute figures, Hobbes
for commonwealth depicts man as compound
sovereignty of an artificial soul
neural reward & punishment
harmony is health, sickness & death of sedition
zealous Mikhailovsky fell on the theory
as the apotheosis of the factory system
mir & the fellowship of the workers'
shelter for the individuality of man

I saw you cry like a ship ready to sail
but nothing happened today that was not like yesterday
we spent the whole day or a walk on the deck or food
herring so sourly I felt shiver all down my back
besides I had three cups of tea without milk
not shake the ship than any railroad train
between coffee & dinner we walked & while walking
we read some passages of Rip Van Winkle & had to stop
a strangled sob story so much & reminded me
return to Russia, I wish you would read it
aloud to mother & Sasha, I'm sure you can get it
in Woodbine, our deck lights, I can see just after dark
& expect to be able to do a lot of writing
in short the first day I have been very happy

the ground is fully prepared for insurrection
not ploughed or tilled or sown for growing food
I expect to settle in Moscow & hope to have you
all here in spring you should not fear coming over
as one you will not be any harm if I resolve
all people here want me to run for Duma
how much will be elected but no one can check
the sagging wooden walls & flaking paint
wood-burning smoky stove & the bare floor
here it will be with me I am sure
the sacredness of every written object
singers with voices too powerful for the room
we do not have cruelty to last forever
we will take part in the summer

seem to recognise that part of the workers
ally with the timorous liberals say
rather than a dangerous one, the result not clear
& in some ways provides each
in the fundamental laws of 1906
Russia in the next, of a constitution
held tsar & his autocratic rule he claims
now he consults with the selected word
parties being legalised (even
the revolutionary socialist parties)
but dumas rebellious dissolved
despite strong presence of gentry
all remaining reforms are cosmetic, the mere
façade system took police regime

a parable is told of warring tribes:
one day a tribesman meets with a magician
who says I will donate whatever you may wish
but the man across the river twice
man responsible stretched out one eye
it's not easy to throw wild ideas
in his complaint the Dutch scholar Erasmus
urged people to unite to end dissension, you
must realise the tremendous strength inherent
that the contract number of a people which opposes
tyranny of the nobility
for the revolution cause written
there is no place for any of the privileges
or the slightest degree of oppression of man by man

here it is, finally got here, the best flour!
we drive more, but found nowhere to work
rooms are empty on the desk phone
if the shell revolvers, machinegun belt
overlap one another's arms & they sit on the floor
supping tea from a cup, herrings & salt crusts of bread
as passengers huddled together in the station
greatcoats & reek of boots, cold-hearted piece
wild rain while the other with hopeless shrugs push through
in a slip road slick with trodden mud & snow
many regiments fought many enemies within
exactly unsure who the enemy may be
I was told the work rapidly goes forward
while others, with sceptical smile, order more story

ah, pessimist, you do not know the people
of crowd by Nevski larger today how always
from the argument it moved further on the invective
to assign red flowers to the law court for their sins
against the people of his proposal they cracked as & whips
the deep incision, cavalry attacked & in turn attack
the scream of dissatisfaction & of stone
chunks of ice to demonstrate toward police crowd animosity
Tseretelli's statement is few & fierce, does not have & simply
their peace is seizes from in & within war
he said that possibly comprehends in each Russian word
– ah, pharaoh, has come your edge! here we destroy
flay the blood onto paving, two bodies, a falling man
from where we stood we look at the incandescence of fire

for the passéists between we, great Apollo
has hoisted a sun glaring over the ways,
the Poets Café, monument to us all,
where a Mauser is found apart from a dish of cakes –
does it not make you happy to feel freely?
does the king of clowns love pregnant men
in a city of justice & inflated breasts; the rumps of horses
too much seems still unfamiliar & unclear
since we still examine the conundra of singers
with voices too powerful for the dancers of the room
not dressed to dance, by an orange wall
before which he sits with red scarf neatly arranged
insane squares you will slay with rhomboids
upon the façades of peeling colonnaded villas

we threw downward from tsar & kow-tow to these
no one gives to us rescuing, not heroes nor gods, the people
as a wall in defence of its things,
saint ikons, vestments, chalices of gold, wing of paper
for the flight into fancies without dull need of boots
the earth is fully prepared for the uprising
without ploughing for the food which increases under plough
or sown but for the bloody resurrection
of fighting-men, under-trod women –
from the tree the mushroom is to a flower
barely of cup raised to bear the gift of rain
occupy of a girl-child to examine the waxy fruit
observe the insect in the midst of nameless
above hear them jays in battle with the crows

number me the things that have not yet been
the Russian peasant commune our existence
revolution our tradition, the village
our legal system, on the order of our ancient
anarchy, the bond between us now
from theory moved to remonstration
the reward of thy whoredom shall be in thy heart
& all your people scattered among the nations
to any other hostile words pay little attention
you see our refuge barren
I was nine years old she wrote when the Okhrana
ripped my mother to Siberia
then were the entrances of the world made narrow
so that of your silence you should come to rest

at 3.15 soldiers, investigators & officials
cut off & descended in the bureau, telephone wire
held Martens, Nuorteva, Heller, Weinstein & Hourwich
short of physical violence in the most severe treatment
ignoring requests of diplomatic immunity
& the order for violation of office cleaning
seized the items unrelated to find very many
aside from correspondence, pamphlets, speeches & files
took cash boxes, briefcases, file cabinets & desks
family photos, the Soviet flag & a Russian velvet hat
however, no warrant & a raid going on
was more dramatic & resulted in front-page press
most governments are viewed as hostile blockade trade show
act of the previous formal declaration of war

pursuant to the instructions of Superintendent Offley
we find that Nicholas Hourvich in 1918
helped shape the plan
for American Red Protection, purpose of which
were sent an emissary to Russia to revolution
& that there is no direct evidence of hand
he allegedly alien, with the boast of
his friendship often with Trotsky & Lenin
went on a long country
speaking in Russian it's not fit to
go into detail his speeches on the nature
is one of the prominent leaders brainiest &
right orator & writer & dangerous
would be under influence in thousands of acolytes

there are differences between countries in the world of multiple classes
in addition to England – I miss the way home in Russia!
there is currently only in my life
a small house a little cottage
the room in which to read the book to read
ten fire & extinguished the lamp
I need to go outside the bedroom so cold
is Kolya married, desperate for news?
come down for breakfast I wanted every morning
letter telling when Clive will come
two months since he left under my angel
& his people but kindly old & English
conditions completely unfit for people
belonging to an educated class

a new economic policy & many
exuded the smell of rotten Thermidor
period of the French degeneration
leaders of opposition & struggle between
obtained heights of bitterness, depths of despair
each part of conspiracy charged in this & other
& betrayal of the revolution, some
by reference to the guillotine's influence
propagandists had often to respond
to be angry with the question of what we fought for?
in a mood of growing belligerence the workers
scented the privileges of the bourgeois to the experts –
Stalin, Trotsky was known to be different,
is not charismatic, intellectual, or Jewish

I no longer believe in the accuracy of my own
& am condemned forever to suffer the errors of others
have cast into the waters all conventions & precepts
so every touch of steering is life & death
every wrong idea we follow the crime committed
against future generations good intention's no interest
only one anchor holds us & faith in self
slightest cause a collision moral short-circuit
thus we derive our mutual destruction
yet how may you determine how to judge
truth in the future? vision or logical deduction?
we do the work of prophets without gift
engineering the realization of the human mind
but those who do not believe the falling buildings

greasy light of the cellar steps, sweat
in & out of breath stained walls & clammy
pale & pustular official flesh
oozing from his neck, easier to infiltrate
for sausage fingers probing in the crevice
padded stuffed husks bulging as soft doors
a soundproofed cell, a chintzy underground
neurosis apparatchik for the treatment
microphones are buried, set in stone
where queasy testimony may amuse
listeners but the game's still bleak
giftless performance of the wayward prophet
rip bridge, the underlying block
that shift and threatened in a shaky state

at last it has come to this: bread, dust, the artillery
stretched through that crystal waterway
our brains which reach the ice of silver burns,
during all our skull ink freezing which are painted
our hands, which are too deaf, the hand-written
nobody-housing building classified by does it burn
& ideas, institution cast into the rage & passion;
to wild search for disentangle; in order to release
seeking them themselves roughly; proclamation
& the law where now paper becomes extinct
revolving in a giant unceasing machine
from the experiment by which existence is hard to withstand
the lie which is included by the mortal cold of the enemy
the wheel of the field which exceeds the city

there is the cool consolation where as for me
already putting out voice in distrustful morning,
everyone who fears awakening the minimum doubt
which you read the following shock which it should expect
threatened when being hardships, forfeit bad ribbon
capital punishment of the typewriter where in any case
because of those of camp illegally adjusts the radio
the good deed of the time of tribulation is this
but & which reads post together with us;
it is that it reaches the point where you are conscious for the second time;
as for writing by pencil, possibility of camouflage
which is permitted in this way, with the Minsk reconstruction
depending upon me who am removed just under the refuge
of at least interesting darkness where the fresh air breathes

but as the flesh fell from his face
vertical pride & bone growth
grey beard & sinks the eye fade
lost without sounding & spark
the full immerse attached spring will survive
living water from natural sources or wells
impure event in some time passes & flow
rainwater must still take its ritual effect
long-fingered hands gentle massage of the forehead
as he peers & pore over the mildewy page
dog's ear & total of old absurd histories
collection of utensils for communicating the past
sanctity of each written object
a sacred protracted taste hope in his lip

blindly believing concrete truths, absolute & release
Moshe, the soldier & the poet
breaks the second instruction, ark
of our spoiled understanding, our holiest things
befouled & profaned, our strong made weak
our glorious house conjunct, level with our desperation
the grapes ripen & what will they tread?
the sway of famine & those who escape
you with blood's hand, your foot fast to make slaughter
am the pebble will be falling, the feast crescent moon
chilly wind the stump will expel the house desolate
objection of his wry smile illusion
Moses did not write the show he was lying
in sky's kingdom similar to the exact ground

never rise the dreamers on desires of the fathers
of our fathers which we longed ourselves human eyes
& blood to the skies, which with stars, a strange view
perfection of yearning, glance of the sun which
is eaten covered, image of the blood light ray
being for the present removed, the range of vision
which bends from oppression, floats dimly
with the air of Chagall's remembered shtetl;
magazine disguises in the head of a boy
where is to the eye which puts on the cloth,
ignition smoke where the room becomes dense,
thin slice where carries all sins which asks;
it does not tear its eyes of the dismembered body
as death wields scythe on the head of the boy

that she came to me in my captivity
we join in the laughter, tears once shed are happy
it's not a word more of love we passed
fear of strangers in these streets from drowning
with the influx of new immigrants to the city
café in the ghettoes' university
inferior jobs all fell to them while older
more experienced workers rose in skill
rank & income that to the eager young was a Utopia
as accurately as possible in the course
of negotiation but myself a man doomed utterly
that swinging a line between audacity & compassion
leave our troubles behind, peel off the fear
that haunts our days & nights

each morning I go down to breakfast hoping
sunset its time fort structure given by the bell
for a minute or two you see nothing so deep gloom
buried with fear of imminent execution or exile
no books or the sordid soap paper in place
later the stench of poison in your own
– how I remember our Russian home!
a great power, the tyranny of decency
Tuesday & ten o'clock lights are off
secret death of a diary he reads
& was the engraver of the offence
a symbol multiplied by hostile tribes
our destroyed houses, conditions quite unsuitable
two months since I left him in Arkhangelsk

it is not breaks the second instruction
religiously observant, choosing to cover her hair
the grapes ripen & what will they tread?
for them, many living in the ground
the sway of famine & those who escape
by gun search & contaminate the house of prayer
in the cool wood the mushrooms are in flower
and came to raise until punishment the cup
no one gives us salvation
not God nor the heroic gothic type
the poet who constructed Torah as a soldier might,
blindly believing specific truth, absolute dance & absolve
what Moshe? soldier and poet –
to even write poetry after Oświęcim is barbaric

long noble massage of hands brow
confirmed in writing as they speak in Minsk
in a twilight era of the old order
unmistakable in decay the new
not yet defined a break in alienation
of the ghetto forced migration
& the spark after impure fact complete immersion
but the rain waters should be still
not well disposed to any sacred writ
heretic among socialist
undernourished landless of the soil
Marxist on Russia's pragmatic member states
the irrational story old passing, the taste
of the instrument which it conveys prolonged

the bone is pulled out, the eye which is dented atrophies,
the spring which has lived flows to become clean
peasants under the same series on how the mere
means of compelling the farmer to work
in the family fundamental sugarcane landless fasting soil
his ironical smile against his fraud
but how the flesh has fallen from his person
standing pride & stature & the sunk eyes weakened
executing ceremony for the calm hand of the long finger
inspect in detail the intended holiness by all documents
where yearning with that lip of the collection
irrational, ragged & of musty page
a young girl cherishes the namelessness
as olives clinging to the tree through winter

& when I had made an end of speaking these words
then left I the meditations wherein I was:
why art thou moved, whereas thou art but mortal?
wherefore weepest thou? why art so grieved in thy mind?
let the multitude perish which was born in vain —
are not the evils which are come to us sufficient?
some things shalt thou secretly reveal to the wise
for wickedness hath exceedingly polluted the earth
therefore write all these things thou hast seen in book & hide them
regard not the wicked inventions of the heathen
who understood the words wherein they were instructed
100 bullocks, 200 rams, 400 lambs
12 goats for the sin of all Israel; & said in their hearts
that there is no god and that knowing they must die

Notes

this Esdras went up

This poem, and the one with which the book concludes, are composed entirely of lines drawn from the two *Books of Esdras*. The same source provided language and ideas for many of the ensuing sonnets. Though not included in the Hebrew Bible, and only among the apocrypha of most Christian ones, the books remain part of the Eastern Orthodox canon.

bent writing, assiduous pen in hand

Isaac Aaronovitch Hourwich (1860-1924) stood unsuccessfully for both the US Congress and the Russian Duma. Born in Vilna, Lithuania, he was educated in St Petersburg, exiled to Siberia, where his eldest son Nicholas was born, then fled to the US. He struggled the rest of his life to support two families, one in New York and one in Russia. Melech Epstein, in his *Profiles of Eleven*, describes IAH as "a peculiar and challenging man".

radicalism is not your mistake

Thermidor was the 11th month in the French revolutionary calendar, the month in 1794 in which Robespierre was guillotined and the Reign of Terror ended. Leon Trotsky, in *The Revolution Betrayed*, describes the rise of Stalin as the "Soviet Thermidor", meaning a retreat from the principles of the revolution.

for them many living on the earth

"They that dwell upon the earth may understand nothing": *II Esdras 4: 21*

our psaltery is laid down on the land

"The ark of our covenant's spoiled, our holy things defiled": *II Esdras 10: 22*

expound, expound, the vinestocks lie untended

A more familiar form of the name Esdras is Ezra. Many of the finest and most influential poets, including a number of Jews, owe an acknowledged debt to Ezra Pound. Thus an anti-Semitic windbag is a significant figure in the development of a partly Jewish aesthetic tradition.

as for us & of art & art

According to a paper read before the Syro-Egyptian society of London on December 17, 1844 by William Holt Yates, "Not a vestige remains of the ancient magnificence of 'On' . . . if we except one solitary monument which has been left, as it were, to denote the departure of Egypt's glory, and to commemorate this ancient seat of learning, the favourite dwelling-place of Pythagoras, Herodotus, Plato, and his friend Eudoxus, a celebrated astronomer, the pupil of Ichonuphy, a priest in the temple of the Sun, of Aristotle and many others ... It is about sixty-seven feet four inches in height and is covered with hieroglyphics ... It is called by the Bedoueens 'The Pillar of Abraham'."

I conducted you through & sea, at the beginning

The speaker of this sonnet and the one following is that same God whose very existence is called into question, even denied, by the more learned characters we will meet.

intention of the blower is critical to hearer

The blowing of the shofar, the ram's horn, is associated primarily with Rosh Hashanah and Yom Kippur. The shofar says, "Wake from your sleep. Become the best person you can." The halakha rules that the shofar may not be sounded on Shabbat.

in shul & bes-medresh we occupy these text

The once beautiful city of Vitebsk in Belarus, where the painter Marc Chagall (Moshe Shagal) was born in 1887, has mistakenly been described as a village. Chagall's work is noted for rays of light and colour, and for the fish motifs he added in honour of his father, who was employed by a herring merchant. His mother sold groceries.

the woodcarving tradition which delivers

The surviving remnants of Aaron Chait's remarkable *Throne of King Solomon*, which he worked on through much of the 1920s, are on permanent exhibition in the Vilna Gaon Museum of Tolerance in Vilnius.

in order not to break the second command

The aron kodesh is a receptacle, or ornamental closet, housing a synagogue's Torah scrolls. The fine closet doors on display at the Vilna Gaon Museum are almost the only surviving relic of that city's Great Synagogue, which survived the Nazis only to be demolished in 1950 under Soviet rule.

the input viewpoint takes truth ignorant & in disguise

Cuneiform script on the so-called 'Cyrus Cylinder' found in the ruins of Babylon in 1879 confirms that Cyrus allowed the captive Israelites to return to their traditional lands, earning his honoured place in the Judaic tradition. It is one of the ironies of the medieval 'blood libel' that Christianity is the only major religion to cherish symbolic cannibalism.

fair reader's desire of the girl's capital

Isaac Hourwich described the circumstances of his eight-month imprisonment as a student in 1879-80 in an article for the July 1901 issue of *Frank Leslie's Popular Monthly*. The piece is subtitled 'A personal narrative which casts much light on the present troubles in St Petersburg'.

Kropotkin settled with a sense of ease in silence

The anarchist Prince Peter Kropotkin escaped in 1875 after 18 months in the Peter and Paul Fortress in St Petersburg, where he enjoyed reading Dickens. Isaac Hourwich had no such luxury when incarcerated there four years later, fully expecting to be executed.

an imperial world's population change

"From early on the Jews were suspected of playing sinister roles in Populist terrorism. [There was a] strongly held belief about 'the complete unity and solidarity of Jews' and the implicit, but fallacious, argument that the Jewish community was responsible for the acts of Jewish terrorists because its leaders willingly, if not purposefully, failed to exercise their authority over Jews who conspired against the state" – Erich H. Haberer, *Jews and Revolution in Nineteenth Century Russia*

the schizoid character of Russian society

"By the end of the [19th] century an individual's self-definition as an *intelligent* often implied relatively passive liberal attitudes" – Sheila Fitzpatrick, *The Russian Revolution*

& masquerade of revellers

On April 28, 1903 the *New York Times* reported, "The anti-Jewish riots in Kishinev, Bessarabia, are worse than the censor will permit to publish. There was a well laid-out plan for the general massacre of Jews on the day following the Russian Easter. The mob was led by priests, and the general cry, 'Kill the Jews,' was taken up all over the city. The Jews were taken wholly unaware and were slaughtered like sheep."

sound of blows began the dream of Vera

My grandmother was nine years old when her mother and aunt were arrested in the night and sent to Siberia. It was several years before she saw either of them again.

Białystok from London on the reading & critique of Talmud

"A unique type of human being, the Jewish intellectual, springs from the tradition of the *talmud hakhem*, the lifelong student. For 2000 years the main energies of Jewish communities in various parts of the world have gone into the mass production of intellectuals" – Harold Rosenberg
"As the Yiddish adage held, *'In Amerike, dertsyen di kinder di eltern'* (in America, the children raise their parents)" – Tony Michels, *A Fire In Their Hearts*

the café is the universities from the ghetto

Born in Keidan, Lithuania, the journalist Bernard Gershon Richards wrote a column for the Boston Evening Post under the pseudonym Keidansky. In his 1903 *Discourses of Keidansky* he provides a colourful portrait of Second Avenue, remarking, 'Why, I have gotten enough ideas on the East Side to last me for ten years'. *Di Tsukunft* (The Future), now 'the world's oldest Yiddish literary journal', began publication in 1892. Early editions featured on its cover the slogan, 'Workers of all countries, unite!'

bay mir bistu sheyn, to me are you

Composer Sholom Secunda and lyricist Jacob Jacobs wrote *Bay mir bistu sheyn* for their 1932 musical *M'ken lebn nor m'lost nit* (I Would If I Could). The song became the biggest hit to emerge from the Yiddish musical theatre of Second Avenue, which flourished from 1882 to about the time of the Second World War. It enjoyed great radio success in Nazi Germany until its origin was revealed. The tune was subsequently used in the Soviet Union for an anti-German propaganda song, *Baron von der Spik*.

my dear Vladimir Ilyich, forgive that I do not address you as comrade

In February 1914 Lenin wrote to Isaac Hourwich thanking him for a copy of his book *Immigration and Labor* and requesting access to more statistical information. Years earlier Lenin, as testified by Trotsky, had made much use of Hourwich's *Economics of the Russian Village*.

the Russian peasant family alone

All the lines from which this and the two following sonnets were carved come originally from Hourwich, *The Economics of the Russian Village*, New York, 1892.

Gleb Oospensky in his suspicion stood alone

Journalist and short-story writer Oospensky's best-known work *The Power of the Land*, based on his studies of life in the city of Nizhny Novgorod on the Volga, was published in 1882. Vera Hourwich was born there in 1890.

for me & not only for me in those days

"One thing had been settled *completely*. We had already known for certain *that we were not Jews*" – Chaim Zhitlovsky

to suffer silence is to suffer as a fool

"To dispose decisively of the question (and degree) of governmental responsibility in all cases of anti-Jewish violence is impossible" – Hans Rogger

the first edition of Leviathan

The link between Hobbes's *Leviathan* and the Populist theories of Mikhailovsky is drawn, somewhat tenuously, by Sir John Maynard in *Russia In Flux*, London 1942

I saw you cry like a ship ready to sail

In March 1906, following the marginal relaxation of the tsarist autocracy in the 1905 revolution, Isaac Hourwich sailed for Europe on the German steamer *Amerika*. Making his way via London, Paris and Switzerland, he arrived at his father's home in Minsk in May. This poem is derived from a letter written to his young daughter Beckie (later known as the author and female activist Rebecca Hourwich Reyher) on his first day at sea.

the ground is fully prepared for insurrection

It is clear from his letters that Isaac Hourwich's primary motive in returning to Russia was the hope of making a better living than he had achieved in New York. The decision to stand for the Duma appears to have come only after his arrival in Minsk. Having passed the first ballot as candidate for the new Democratic People's Party, his election was annulled by the senate in St Petersburg. He returned in 1907 to New York, and his American family.
Fungi have cryptic lifestyles. A mushroom is considered as a fruiting body, but has no flower.

seem to recognise that part of the workers

After the Duma elections the leaders of the various socialist parties, most of whom had returned to Russia during or shortly after the

1905 revolution, were forced back into emigration to avoid imprisonment or exile.

a parable is told of warring tribes

"The great October Socialist Revolution itself and Lenin's teachings affirm the national distinctiveness of art, literature and Soviet culture in general. So against whom should we fight, and what for?" – Rasul Gamzatov, *Fidelity To Talent*, quoted in *One Hundred Nationalities, One People*, by Eduard Bagramov, Moscow 1982

here it is finally got here, the best flour

In the early days of the 1917 revolution, logistics was one of the major issues; not only the movement of men and women, but of materials, including basic foodstuffs such as flour. The account here comes largely from Pitirim Sorokin, Kerensky's secretary in the government of February to October 1917, who went on to found the sociology department at Harvard. He had a particular interest in altruism.

ah, pessimist, you do not know the people

The account of Menshevik leader Irakli Tseretelli's speech to the Constituent Assembly in Petrograd on January 18, 1918, comes from Edgar Sisson, President Woodrow Wilson's Special Representative.

for the passéists between we, great Apollo

In November 1917, in the first weeks after the Bolshevik Revolution, the Futurist poet Vasily Kamensky persuaded the confectioner Dmitri Filipov to subsidise a small café for poets in a disused Moscow laundry. Historian W Bruce Lincoln writes, in *Red Victory*, "Everything and everyone connected with art in Moscow came together at the Poets' Café . . . David Burliuk and his Cubist friends smeared the walls with black paint, over which they emblazoned an array of swollen female torsos and many-legged horses' rumps."

we threw downward from tsar & kow-tow to these

"We have cast down the Tsar and subjected ourselves to Jews. The Russian people . . . are forging for themselves Jewish-Masonic slavery" – delegate to the Church Council of Russia, January 1918

number me the things that have not yet been

The revolutionary tradition in Russia, kept alive among students and the intelligentsia, dates from the Decembrist revolt of 1825.

at 3.15 soldiers, investigators & officials

On June 12, 1919, the Russian Soviet Bureau in New York City was raided by officers representing the Lusk Committee, or Joint Legislative Committee to Investigate Seditious Activities. The bureau had been set up by Russia's new Bolshevik government to try to secure diplomatic recognition by the United States. Isaac Hourwich was head of the bureau's department of economics and statistics and was standing in for Morris Hillquit, who was unwell, as acting director of the legal department.

pursuant to the instructions of Superintendent Offley

From a special statement of operational evidence filed by FBI agent MJ Davis in New York City on July 7, 1919. Davis reports: "Hourvich has been one of the leaders who have agitated for the adoption of 'Bolshevik' principles by the American Socialist Party." He concludes: "A special effort is being made to obtain documentary evidence of Hourvitz' citizenship."

there are differences between countries in the world of multiple classes

In November 1919, two months after a hasty marriage enabled her to escape from Russia's civil war, Vera Hourwich Semmens wrote to her sister Manya in New York from the home of her new in-laws in Kent, "I don't think that there is any other country where class differences are felt so much as in England."

a new economic policy & many

The NEP, brought in by Lenin in 1921 as "a strategic retreat" from revolutionary Communist principles, led to a rapid and much-needed economic recovery. Abandoned by Stalin, it later became known as "the Bukharin alternative".

I no longer believe in the accuracy of my own

The portrayal of the fallen Rubashov in *Darkness at Noon* by Arthur Koestler parallels uncannily much of what I have been able to learn or surmise of the fate of Isaac Hourwich's son Nicholas, who died suddenly in Moscow in 1934, supposedly of a heart attack. Nick, as he was known in the US (Kolya in Russia and to his family), was a founding leader of the Communist Party of the USA and American delegate to the second and third Comintern World Congresses in Moscow in 1920 and 1921. He is said to have argued with Lenin there and never again left Russia.

greasy light of the cellar steps

The KGB prison in Vilnius preserves the underground cells in which political prisoners were held in solitary confinement, interrogated, tortured and shot. No doubt the basement of the infamous Lubyanka in Moscow was similar, though much larger.

at last it has come to this

The Leningrad siege diaries of Vera Inber, like the Dresden diaries of Victor Klemperer (next sonnet) have no real place in this narrative yet simply wouldn't keep out. All that follows is what follows.

it is not breaks the second instruction

Theodor Adorno's famous proscription against writing poetry post-Auschwitz, while understandable in its time, would if followed hand a small but crucial victory to the Nazis. (It is for this reason that Adorno himself later retracted it.) The Shoah made it much more difficult, but no less vital, to bear witness to the culture it was intended to eradicate; and not merely to preserve traditions, but continue them. I have attempted throughout this sequence to honour and continue the post-theistic Jewish tradition of my forebears as well as the aesthetic spirit of the Poets' Café.

& when I had made an end

There is disagreement as to whether the original language of the *Books of Esdras* was Greek, Aramaic or Hebrew. The English translation of 1611 was based on both Greek and Latin texts.

a note on the translation

Brought up to speak Russian, Isaac Hourwich learned both English and Yiddish in order to communicate effectively as lawyer, journalist, lecturer and statistician in the USA. Vera (Hourwich) Semmens, his daughter and my grandmother, was adept enough at these and other languages to serve as an interpreter at the Nuremburg Trials. She would be appalled at the mistranslations which these once more-or-less regular sonnets have undergone.

Acknowledgments

Poems in the current collection have appeared in print or online in *Blackbox Manifold, Free Verse, Notre Dame Review, Otoliths, Pirene's Fountain, Shadowtrain, Shearsman* and *Stride* magazines. I am indebted to Mark Donnelly and Abby Hourwich for sharing with me some of the research upon which these poems are based.

About the Author

As a student at Cambridge University in the 1970s, Aidan Semmens was chairman of the Cambridge Poetry Society, co-editor of the influential *Perfect Bound* magazine and winner of the Chancellor's Medal for an English Poem in 1978, the same year his first pamphlet of verse appeared in print in the UK. After that, like his poetic hero George Oppen, he stopped writing poetry for some years. Since he resumed, his poems have appeared in print and online in magazines including *Jacket, Jack, Shearsman, Shadowtrain, Stride, Great Works, Free Verse, Blackbox Manifold, Likestarlings, Poetry Wales, Tears In The Fence* and *Notre Dame Review.* His first full-length collection, *A Stone Dog,* was published by Shearsman Books in 2011. He has also edited an anthology of poetry from the English county of Suffolk, *By The North Sea,* for publication in 2013.

Away from poetry, he works as a freelance journalist, contributing mostly sports reports to British regional and national newspapers; he also exhibits and sells some of his photographs.

Free Verse Editions

Edited by Jon Thompson

13 ways of happily by Emily Carr
Between the Twilight and the Sky by Jennie Neighbors
Blood Orbits by Ger Killeen
The Bodies by Chris Sindt
The Book of Isaac by Aidan Semmens
Canticle of the Night Path by Jennifer Atkinson
Child in the Road by Cindy Savett
Contrapuntal by Christopher Kondrich
Country Album by James Capozzi
The Curiosities by Brittany Perham
Current by Lisa Fishman
Divination Machine by F. Daniel Rzicznek
Erros by Morgan Lucas Schuldt
The Forever Notes by Ethel Rackin
The Flying House by Dawn-Michelle Baude
Instances: Selected Poems by Jeongrye Choi, translated by Brenda Hill-
     man, Wayne de Fremery, and Jeongrye Choi
A Map of Faring by Peter Riley
Physis by Nicolas Pesque, translated by Cole Swensen
Poems from above the Hill & Selected Work by Ashur Etwebi, translated
     by Brenda Hillman and Diallah Haidar
The Prison Poems by Miguel Hernández, translated by Michael Smith
Puppet Wardrobe by Daniel Tiffany
Quarry by Carolyn Guinzio
remanence by Boyer Rickel
Signs Following by Ger Killeen
These Beautiful Limits by Thomas Lisk
An Unchanging Blue: Selected Poems 1962–1975 by Rolf Dieter Brink-
     mann, translated by Mark Terrill
Under the Quick by Molly Bendall
Verge by Morgan Lucas Schuldt
The Wash by Adam Clay
We'll See by George Godeau, translated by Kathleen McGookey
What Stillness Illuminated by Yermiyahu Ahron Taub
Winter Journey [Viaggio d'inverno] by Attilio Bertolucci, translated by
     Nicholas Benson

www.ingramcontent.com/pod-product-compliance
Lightning Source LLC
Chambersburg PA
CBHW032028090426
42741CB00006B/766